Focus on Purpose, Not Fear

365 Scriptures about Fear

One for Each Day of the Year

Rev. Harris D. McFarlane

DEDICATION

To my wife, Jennifer, the woman who is both my dream come true and my best friend. When God gave you to me, he gave me the best. Your support, love, dedication, and encouragement have shaped me into the man that I am today. I love you very much!

To my daughter, Nicole, you have brought so much joy, love, purpose, and passion into my life. Being your dad is my greatest and most treasured reward.

I love you!

with love

INTRODUCTION

Moving beyond fear is a meticulous, and fundamental part of accomplishing our God-given purpose. We're all afraid of something: starting, finishing, changing direction, taking risks, etc. Fear can limit our growth, block our creativity, limit our success, deteriorate our relationships, and paralyze our potential. Fear can also rob us of our purpose and mission. It keeps us from becoming all that we can be, and stops us from becoming all that God has designed and ordained for us to be. Simply put, fear can hold us back from God's best intentions and plans and can prevent us from finding his meaning and purpose for our lives.

"For the thing which I greatly feared is come upon me, and that which I was afraid of is come unto me." Job 3:25

Instead, consider the alternative, "that which I have passion for and expect with unwavering faith, come into existence." Vividly visualize what you desire, and begin to act with faith, purpose, belief, and expectation. God in His wisdom created us in His own image to enjoy a relationship with Him and planned for our life to be filled with meaning and purpose. As such, it is important we focus on purpose and never fear.

William Shakespeare said, "Our doubts are traitors, and make us lose the good we oft might win, by fearing to attempt."

Fear holds us back. Fear is a lack of faith in the promises of God.

Psychologists have identified numerous kinds of fears that can block, limit, or hinder humans from growing, becoming, achieving, and accomplishing. Some of these prominent fears are the: fear of failure, fear of the unknown, fear of criticism, fear of success, fear of what other people think, fear of rejection, fear of old age, fear of death, fear of losing control, fear of poverty, fear of ill health, fear of loss of love, fear of being disappointed, and fear of change. If fear is not confronted and dealt with, it can take our happiness, confidence, security, peace of mind, and purpose. Fear can limit us from making fresh starts and stepping out into unchartered territories. For example, the children of Israel were kept out of the Promised Land because they were afraid, insecure, timid, and doubtful. This caused them to spend forty years wandering around the wilderness.

Zechariah and Elizabeth, without a doubt, had prayed for many years to have a baby, but it didn't happen within the time frame they expected. They had numerous setbacks and disappointments. But when Zechariah received the news that Elizabeth was pregnant, his reaction was one of disbelief, doubt, and fear. He was too afraid to elevate his beliefs and expectations. When you allow your thoughts, feelings, decisions to be controlled by fear, you will become a victim of fear.

Fear can place self-imposed limitations and keep you from experiencing the abundant blessings and favors of God.

We're all afraid of something on this broken planet. The antidote to fear is to base your life instead, on the promises of God. The promises of God will never let you down, unlike human promises that are often broken. Resolutions do not last. Goals are often not accomplished. Human plans will often be changed.

However, the promises of God will never fail.

"For all the promises of God in him are yea, and in him Amen, unto the glory of God by us." 2 Corinthians 1:20

Faith, hope, trust, joy, peace, love, and truth cannot be built on what one thinks or what one feels. It must be built and based upon the promises of God. To help you eliminate fear you must: feed your mind with God's truths that have stood the test of time and will last forever. You must, memorize scriptures, claim the promises of God, expect the best, step out in faith, be thankful, follow God's command for us to "fear not," but when you are afraid, depend upon him, believe in him, and know that he always walks with you, and trust him solely. No longer be the prisoner of fear. For example: "what time I am afraid, I will trust in thee." Psalm 56:3

"He shall cover thee with his feathers, and under his wings shall thou trust: his truth shall be thy shield and buckler." Psalm 91:4

When you acknowledge God's promises, you surrender your plans and yourself to Him. Listen attentively unto His voice, adore and praise Him, pray often, and fill your life with truth. When you step out in faith, when you believe and depend upon God, these actions will banish fear.

Crossing the Jordan River was a vital event in Israel's history. Crossing the Red Sea changed Israel's standing from slavery to freedom. By passing through the Jordan River into the Promised Land, it emancipated Israel from a wandering people into an established nation. Yet, to the people, the river seemed like an insurmountable dilemma.

"With men this is impossible; but with God all things are possible." Matthew 19:26

The same God that was with Joshua and the Israelites when they were crossing the Jordan River is the same God that is with us. You must act as if you cannot fail while trusting in God, loving God, and depending on God. You must expect Him to work on your behalf. That is what it means to have faith. It means moving ahead despite your fears. Choosing to do the thing you fear the most. When you do this, the death of fear will be certain. You must focus on purpose and never fear. "When thou passeth through the waters, I will be with thee; and through the rivers, they shall not overflow thee: when thou walkest through the fire, thou shalt not be burned; neither shall the flame kindle upon thee." Isaiah 43:2

This marvelous book that you hold in your hands will help you eliminate all of your deep-rooted fears and start you on a fresh journey toward: confidence, freedom, peace of mind, knowing God better, loving God more, and help take you into the realm of a personal relationship with God.

"One with God is a majority." –Martin Luther.

As you are reading this book, God is compelling you to do something that you have never done before. He is compelling you to reach your highest and most desired destination in what you are seeking to accomplish.

When it is the all-knowing God telling you "do not fear" it is an amazing, powerful, and incredible guide. 365 Scriptures about Fear is one of the most powerful possessions you now have at your disposal. Knowing and using these scriptures can help you in every facet of your life including fostering: wisdom, peace, forgiveness, love, joy, hope, health, and faith.

God wants you to be in control of your fear. You can surely break free from your fears, make a fresh start and fulfill the plan and purpose God has ordained for you because as stated by Psalm 56:3 "what time I am afraid, I will trust in thee." There is a promise in the Bible for every common fear. When you know what God has promised, your fears will disappear.

"The only thing we have to fear is fear itself."–Franklin Delano Roosevelt

"There is only one thing that makes a dream impossible to achieve: the Fear of Failure."–Paul Coelho, Author

"The Great aim of education is not knowledge but action."–Herbert Spencer

These 365 scriptures about fear, one for each day of the year, initiate a breathtaking journey that will transform, renew, and elevate your life to new dimensions. Seize the moment so this extraordinary journey can help you fulfill your life's purpose.

This is not a substitute for the Bible. It is a reminder, guide, and direction to some of the most amazing scriptures about fear taken from the King James Version of the Bible.

I wish every reader an awakening, transformation, elevation, breakthrough, and many miracles in your spiritual, emotional, mental, social, economic, personal, relational, and physical life.

"For God hath not given us the spirit of fear; but of power, and of love, and of a sound mind." 2 Timothy 1:7

365 Scriptures About Fear

1. "What man is he that feareth the Lord? him shall he teach in the way that he shall choose." (Psalm 25:12)

2. "Fear thou not; for I am with thee: be not dismayed; for I am thy God: I will strengthen thee; yea, I will help thee; yea, I will uphold thee with the right hand of my righteousness." (Isaiah 41:10)

3. "Have not I commanded thee? Be strong and of a good courage; be not afraid, neither be thou dismayed: for the Lord thy God is with thee whithersoever thou goest." (Joshua 1:9)

4. "For I the Lord thy God will hold thy right hand, saying unto thee, Fear not; I will help thee." (Isaiah 41:13)

5. "There is no fear in love; but perfect love casteth out fear: because fear hath torment. He that feareth is not made perfect in love." (1 John 4:18)

6. "Yea, though I walk through the valley of the shadow of death, I will fear no evil: for thou art with me; thy rod and thy staff they comfort me." (Psalm 23:4)

7. "The fear of man bringeth a snare: but whoso putteth his trust in the Lord shall be safe." (Proverbs 29:25)

8. "She is not afraid of the snow for her household: for all her household are clothed with scarlet." (Proverbs 31:21)

9. "The Lord is my light and my salvation; whom shall I fear? the Lord is the strength of my life; of whom shall I be afraid? When the wicked, even mine enemies and my foes, came upon me to eat up my flesh, they stumbled and fell. Though an host should encamp against me, my heart shall not fear: though war should rise against me, in this will I be confident." (Psalm 27:1-3)

10. "I sought the Lord, and he heard me, and delivered me from all my fears. They looked unto him, and were lightened: and their faces were not ashamed." (Psalm 34:4-5)

11. "Be strong and of a good courage, fear not, nor be afraid of them: for the Lord thy God, he it is that doth go with thee; he will not fail thee, nor forsake thee." (Deuteronomy 31:6)

12. "And the Lord, he it is that doth go before thee; he will be with thee, he will not fail thee, neither forsake thee: fear not, neither be dismayed." (Deuteronomy 31:8)

13. "For ye have not received the spirit of bondage again to fear; but ye have received the Spirit of adoption, whereby we cry, Abba, Father." (Romans 8:15)

14. "Are not two sparrows sold for a farthing? and one of them shall not fall on the ground without your Father. But the very hairs of your head are all numbered. Fear ye not therefore, ye are of more value than many sparrows." (Matthew 10:29-31)

15. "So that we may boldly say, The Lord is my helper, and I will not fear what man shall do unto me." (Hebrews 13:6)

16. "Take thou no usury of him, or increase: but fear thy God; that thy brother may live with thee." (Leviticus 25:36)

17. "But and if ye suffer for righteousness' sake, happy are ye: and be not afraid of their terror, neither be troubled." (1 Peter 3:14)

18. "Fear not, little flock; for it is your Father's good pleasure to give you the kingdom." (Luke 12:32)

19. "In God I will praise his word, in God I have put my trust; I will not fear what flesh can do unto me." (Psalm 56:4)

20. "Like as a father pitieth his children, so the Lord pitieth them that fear him." (Psalm 103:13)

21. "And the angel said unto her, Fear not, Mary: for thou hast found favour with God. And, behold, thou shalt conceive in thy womb, and bring forth a son, and shalt call his name Jesus." (Luke 1:30-31)

22. "But now thus saith the Lord that created thee, O Jacob, and he that formed thee, O Israel, Fear not: for I have redeemed thee, I have called thee by thy name; thou art mine. When thou passest through the waters, I will be with thee; and through the rivers, they shall not overflow thee: when thou walkest through the fire, thou shalt not be burned; neither shall the flame kindle upon thee. For I am the Lord thy God, the Holy One of Israel, thy Saviour: I gave Egypt for thy ransom, Ethiopia and Seba for thee." (Isaiah 43:1-3)

23. "The fear of the Lord tendeth to life: and he that hath it shall abide satisfied; he shall not be visited with evil." (Proverbs 19:23)

24. "For the thing which I greatly feared is come upon me, and that which I was afraid of is come unto me." (Job 3:25)

25. "Then the same day at evening, being the first day of the week, when the doors were shut where the disciples were assembled for fear of the Jews, came Jesus and stood in the midst, and saith unto them, Peace be unto you." (John 20:19)

26. "After these things the word of the Lord came unto Abram in a vision, saying, Fear not, Abram: I am thy shield, and thy exceeding great reward." (Genesis 15:1)

27. "And Moses said unto the people, Fear ye not, stand still, and see the salvation of the Lord, which he will shew to you today: for the Egyptians whom ye have seen today, ye shall see them again no more forever." (Exodus 14:13)

28. "And I will give peace in the land, and ye shall lie down, and none shall make you afraid: and I will rid evil beasts out of the land, neither shall the sword go through your land." (Leviticus 26:6)

29. "Ye shall not fear them: for the Lord your God he shall fight for you." (Deuteronomy 3:22)

30. "Thou shalt not be afraid of them: but shalt well remember what the Lord thy God did unto Pharaoh, and unto all Egypt." (Deuteronomy 7:18)

31. "And shall say unto them, Hear, O Israel, ye approach this day unto battle against your enemies: let not your hearts faint, fear not, and do not tremble, neither be ye terrified because of them." (Deuteronomy 20:3)

32. "And the Lord said unto Joshua, Fear them not: for I have delivered them into thine hand; there shall not a man of them stand before thee." (Joshua 10:8)

33. "And the Lord said unto Joshua, Be not afraid because of them: for tomorrow about this time will I deliver them up all slain before Israel: thou shalt hough their horses, and burn their chariots with fire." (Joshua 11:6)

34. "And Jael went out to meet Sisera, and said unto him, Turn in, my lord, turn in to me; fear not. And when he had turned in unto her into the tent, she covered him with a mantle." (Judges 4:18)

35. "And the angel of the Lord said unto Elijah, Go down with him: be not afraid of him. And he arose, and went down with him unto the king." (2 Kings 1:15)

36. "And he answered, Fear not: for they that be with us are more than they that be with them." (2 Kings 6:16)

37. "And he said, Hearken ye, all Judah, and ye inhabitants of Jerusalem, and thou king Jehoshaphat, Thus saith the Lord unto you, Be not afraid nor dismayed by reason of this great multitude; for the battle is not yours, but God's." (2 Chronicles 20:15)

38. "Ye shall not need to fight in this battle: set yourselves, stand ye still, and see the salvation of the Lord with you, O Judah and Jerusalem: fear not, nor be dismayed; tomorrow go out against them: for the Lord will be with you." (2 Chronicles 20:17)

39. "And I looked, and rose up, and said unto the nobles, and to the rulers, and to the rest of the people, Be not ye afraid of them: remember the Lord, which is great and terrible, and fight for your brethren, your sons, and your daughters, your wives, and your houses." (Nehemiah 4:14)

40. "And he said unto them, Where is your faith? And they being afraid wondered, saying one to another, What manner of man is this! for he commandeth even the winds and water, and they obey him." (Luke 8:25)

41. "For then shalt thou lift up thy face without spot; yea, thou shalt be stedfast, and shalt not fear." (Job 11:15)

42. "Be not thou afraid when one is made rich, when the glory of his house is increased." (Psalm 49:16)

43. "In God have I put my trust: I will not be afraid what man can do unto me." (Psalm 56:11)

44. "And he led them on safely, so that they feared not: but the sea overwhelmed their enemies." (Psalm 78:53)

45. "Therefore thus saith the Lord God of hosts, O my people that dwellest in Zion, be not afraid of the Assyrian: he shall smite thee with a rod, and shall lift up his staff against thee, after the manner of Egypt." (Isaiah 10:24)

46. "The cities of Aroer are forsaken: they shall be for flocks, which shall lie down, and none shall make them afraid." (Isaiah 17:2)

47. "Say to them that are of a fearful heart, Be strong, fear not: behold, your God will come with vengeance, even God with a recompence; he will come and save you." (Isaiah 35:4)

48. "And Isaiah said unto them, Thus shall ye say unto your master, Thus saith the Lord, Be not afraid of the words that thou hast heard, wherewith the servants of the king of Assyria have blasphemed me." (Isaiah 37:6)

49. "O Zion, that bringest good tidings, get thee up into the high mountain; O Jerusalem, that bringest good tidings, lift up thy voice with strength; lift it up, be not afraid; say unto the cities of Judah, Behold your God!"
(Isaiah 40:9)

50. "Fear not: for I am with thee: I will bring thy seed from the east, and gather thee from the west;" (Isaiah 43:5)

51. "Thus saith the Lord that made thee, and formed thee from the womb, which will help thee; Fear not, O Jacob, my servant; and thou, Jesurun, whom I have chosen." (Isaiah 44:2)

52. "They are upright as the palm tree, but speak not: they must needs be borne, because they cannot go. Be not afraid of them; for they cannot do evil, neither also is it in them to do good." (Jeremiah 10:5)

53. "Therefore fear thou not, O my servant Jacob, saith the Lord; neither be dismayed, O Israel: for, lo, I will save thee from afar, and thy seed from the land of their captivity; and Jacob shall return, and shall be in rest, and be quiet, and none shall make him afraid." (Jeremiah 30:10)

54. "And Gedaliah the son of Ahikam the son of Shaphan sware unto them and to their men, saying, Fear not to serve the Chaldeans: dwell in the land, and serve the king of Babylon, and it shall be well with you." (Jeremiah 40:9)

55. "And said, O man greatly beloved, fear not: peace be unto thee, be strong, yea, be strong. And when he had spoken unto me, I was strengthened, and said, Let my lord speak; for thou hast strengthened me." (Daniel 10:19)

56. "Fear not, O land; be glad and rejoice: for the Lord will do great things. Be not afraid, ye beasts of the field: for the pastures of the wilderness do spring, for the tree beareth her fruit, the fig tree and the vine do yield their strength." (Joel 2:21-22)

57. "According to the word that I covenanted with you when ye came out of Egypt, so my spirit remaineth among you: fear ye not." (Haggai 2:5)

58. "As soon as Jesus heard the word that was spoken, he saith unto the ruler of the synagogue, Be not afraid, only believe." (Mark 5:36)

59. "For they all saw him, and were troubled. And immediately he talked with them, and saith unto them, Be of good cheer: it is I; be not afraid." (Mark 6:50)

60. "And I say unto you my friends, Be not afraid of them that kill the body, and after that have no more that they can do. But I will forewarn you whom ye shall fear: Fear him, which after he hath killed hath power to cast into hell; yea, I say unto you, Fear him." (Luke 12:4-5)

61. "Peace I leave with you, my peace I give unto you: not as the world giveth, give I unto you. Let not your heart be troubled, neither let it be afraid." (John 14:27)

62. "Then spake the Lord to Paul in the night by a vision, Be not afraid, but speak, and hold not thy peace: For I am with thee, and no man shall set on thee to hurt thee: for I have much people in this city." (Acts 18:9-10)

63. "Saying, Fear not, Paul; thou must be brought before Caesar: and, lo, God hath given thee all them that sail with thee." (Acts 27:24)

64. "Even as Sara obeyed Abraham, calling him lord: whose daughters ye are, as long as ye do well, and are not afraid with any amazement." (1 Peter 3:6)

65. "Fear none of those things which thou shalt suffer: behold, the devil shall cast some of you into prison, that ye may be tried; and ye shall have tribulation ten days: be thou faithful unto death, and I will give thee a crown of life." (Revelation 2:10)

66. "And he said, I am God, the God of thy father: fear not to go down into Egypt; for I will there make of thee a great nation." (Genesis 46:3)

67. "Only rebel not ye against the Lord, neither fear ye the people of the land; for they are bread for us: their defence is departed from them, and the Lord is with us: fear them not." (Numbers 14:9)

68. "And the Lord said unto Moses, Fear him not: for I have delivered him into thy hand, and all his people, and his land; and thou shalt do to him as thou didst unto Sihon king of the Amorites, which dwelt at Heshbon." (Numbers 21:34)

69. "When thou goest out to battle against thine enemies, and seest horses, and chariots, and a people more than thou, be not afraid of them: for the Lord thy God is with thee, which brought thee up out of the land of Egypt." (Deuteronomy 20:1)

70. "And the Lord said unto him, Peace be unto thee; fear not: thou shalt not die." (Judges 6:23)

71. "Abide thou with me, fear not: for he that seeketh my life seeketh thy life: but with me thou shalt be in safeguard." (1 Samuel 22:23)

72. "And David said unto him, Fear not: for I will surely shew thee kindness for Jonathan thy father's sake, and will restore thee all the land of Saul thy father; and thou shalt eat bread at my table continually." (2 Samuel 9:7)

73. "And Gedaliah sware to them, and to their men, and said unto them, Fear not to be the servants of the Chaldees: dwell in the land, and serve the king of Babylon; and it shall be well with you." (2 Kings 25:24)

74. "Be strong and courageous, be not afraid nor dismayed for the king of Assyria, nor for all the multitude that is with him: for there be more with us than with him."
(2 Chronicles 32:7)

75. "Their houses are safe from fear, neither is the rod of God upon them." (Job 21:9)

76. "For in the multitude of dreams and many words there are also divers vanities: but fear thou God." (Ecclesiastes 5:7)

77. "When thou liest down, thou shalt not be afraid: yea, thou shalt lie down, and thy sleep shall be sweet." (Proverbs 3:24)

78. "Be not afraid of sudden fear, neither of the desolation of the wicked, when it cometh. For the Lord shall be thy confidence, and shall keep thy foot from being taken." (Proverbs 3:25-26)

79. "Then would I speak, and not fear him; but it is not so with me." (Job 9:35)

80. "Fear not, thou worm Jacob, and ye men of Israel; I will help thee, saith the Lord, and thy redeemer, the Holy One of Israel." (Isaiah 41:14)

81. "In righteousness shalt thou be established: thou shalt be far from oppression; for thou shalt not fear: and from terror; for it shall not come near thee." (Isaiah 54:14)

82. "Ye shall walk after the Lord your God, and fear him, and keep his commandments, and obey his voice, and ye shall serve him, and cleave unto him." (Deuteronomy 13:4)

83. "As an adamant harder than flint have, I made thy forehead: fear them not, neither be dismayed at their looks, though they be a rebellious house." (Ezekiel 3:9)

84. "Then said he unto me, Fear not, Daniel: for from the first day that thou didst set thine heart to understand, and to chasten thyself before thy God, thy words were heard, and I am come for thy words." (Daniel 10:12)

85. "In that day it shall be said to Jerusalem, Fear thou not: and to Zion, Let not thine hands be slack." (Zephaniah 3:16)

86. "And it shall come to pass, that as ye were a curse among the heathen, O house of Judah, and house of Israel; so will I save you, and ye shall be a blessing: fear not, but let your hands be strong." (Zechariah 8:13)

87. "When he raiseth up himself, the mighty are afraid: by reason of breakings they purify themselves." (Job 41:25)

88. "And I will come near to you to judgment; and I will be a swift witness against the sorcerers, and against the adulterers, and against false swearers, and against those that oppress the hireling in his wages, the widow, and the fatherless, and that turn aside the stranger from his right, and fear not me, saith the Lord of hosts." (Malachi 3:5)

89. "But while he thought on these things, behold, the angel of the Lord appeared unto him in a dream, saying, Joseph, thou son of David, fear not to take unto thee Mary thy wife: for that which is conceived in her is of the Holy Ghost." (Matthew 1:20)

90. "And God heard the voice of the lad; and the angel of God called to Hagar out of heaven, and said unto her, What aileth thee, Hagar? fear not; for God hath heard the voice of the lad where he is." (Genesis 21:17)

91. "And the Lord appeared unto him the same night, and said, I am the God of Abraham thy father: fear not, for I am with thee, and will bless thee, and multiply thy seed for my servant Abraham's sake." (Genesis 26:24)

92. "And it came to pass, when she was in hard labour, that the midwife said unto her, Fear not; thou shalt have this son also." (Genesis 35:17)

93. "And he said, Peace be to you, fear not: your God, and the God of your father, hath given you treasure in your sacks: I had your money. And he brought Simeon out unto them." (Genesis 43:23)

94. "And Joseph said unto them, Fear not: for am I in the place of God?" (Genesis 50:19)

95. "Now therefore fear ye not: I will nourish you, and your little ones. And he comforted them, and spake kindly unto them." (Genesis 50:21)

96. "And Moses said unto the people, Fear not: for God is come to prove you, and that his fear may be before your faces, that ye sin not." (Exodus 20:20)

97. "Ye shall not respect persons in judgment; but ye shall hear the small as well as the great; ye shall not be afraid of the face of man; for the judgment is God's: and the cause that is too hard for you, bring it unto me, and I will hear it." (Deuteronomy 1:17)

98. "Behold, the Lord thy God hath set the land before thee: go up and possess it, as the Lord God of thy fathers hath said unto thee; fear not, neither be discouraged." (Deuteronomy 1:21)

99. "And when Aaron and all the children of Israel saw Moses, behold, the skin of his face shone; and they were afraid to come nigh him." (Exodus 34:30)

100. "And the Lord said unto me, Fear him not: for I will deliver him, and all his people, and his land, into thy hand; and thou shalt do unto him as thou didst unto Sihon king of the Amorites, which dwelt at Heshbon." (Deuteronomy 3:2)

101. "And the Lord said unto Joshua, Fear not, neither be thou dismayed: take all the people of war with thee, and arise, go up to Ai: see, I have given into thy hand the king of Ai, and his people, and his city, and his land." (Joshua 8:1)

102. "And Joshua said unto them, Fear not, nor be dismayed, be strong and of good courage: for thus shall the Lord do to all your enemies against whom ye fight." (Joshua 10:25)

103. "And about the time of her death the women that stood by her said unto her, Fear not; for thou hast born a son. But she answered not, neither did she regard it." (1 Samuel 4:20)

104. "And he said unto him, Fear not: for the hand of Saul my father shall not find thee; and thou shalt be king over Israel, and I shall be next unto thee; and that also Saul my father knoweth." (1 Samuel 23:17)

105. "And Elijah said unto her, Fear not; go and do as thou hast said: but make me thereof a little cake first, and bring it unto me, and after make for thee and for thy son." (1 Kings 17:13)

106. "And David said to Solomon his son, Be strong and of good courage, and do it: fear not, nor be dismayed: for the Lord God, even my God, will be with thee; he will not fail thee, nor forsake thee, until thou hast finished all the work for the service of the house of the Lord." (1 Chronicles 28:20)

107. "I will not be afraid of ten thousands of people, that have set themselves against me round about." (Psalm 3:6)

108. "And it shall be with him, and he shall read therein all the days of his life: that he may learn to fear the Lord his God, to keep all the words of this law and these statutes, to do them." (Deuteronomy 17:19)

109. "Fear ye not, neither be afraid: have not I told thee from that time, and have declared it? ye are even my witnesses. Is there a God beside me? yea, there is no God; I know not any." (Isaiah 44:8)

110. "Hearken unto me, ye that know righteousness, the people in whose heart is my law; fear ye not the reproach of men, neither be ye afraid of their revilings." (Isaiah 51:7)

111. "Behold, my terror shall not make thee afraid, neither shall my hand be heavy upon thee." (Job 33:7)

112. "Fear thou not, O Jacob my servant, saith the Lord: for I am with thee; for I will make a full end of all the nations whither I have driven thee: but I will not make a full end of thee, but correct thee in measure; yet will I not leave thee wholly unpunished." (Jeremiah 46:28)

113. "Upon earth there is not his like, who is made without fear." (Job 41:33)

114. "And I said unto you, I am the Lord your God; fear not the gods of the Amorites, in whose land ye dwell: but ye have not obeyed my voice." (Judges 6:10)

115. "And now, my daughter, fear not; I will do to thee all that thou requirest: for all the city of my people doth know that thou art a virtuous woman." (Ruth 3:11)

116. "And Samuel said unto the people, Fear not: ye have done all this wickedness: yet turn not aside from following the Lord, but serve the Lord with all your heart." (1 Samuel 12:20)

117. "Afterward shall the children of Israel return, and seek the Lord their God, and David their king; and shall fear the Lord and his goodness in the latter days." (Hosea 3:5)

118. "Let those that fear thee turn unto me, and those that have known thy testimonies." (Psalm 119:79)

119. "And when the disciples saw him walking on the sea, they were troubled, saying, It is a spirit; and they cried out for fear. But straightway Jesus spake unto them, saying, Be of good cheer; it is I; be not afraid." (Matthew 14:26-27)

120. "And the angel said unto them, Fear not: for, behold, I bring you good tidings of great joy, which shall be to all people. For unto you is born this day in the city of David a Saviour, which is Christ the Lord." (Luke 2:10-11)

121. "So when they had rowed about five and twenty or thirty furlongs, they see Jesus walking on the sea, and drawing nigh unto the ship: and they were afraid. But he saith unto them, It is I; be not afraid." (John 6:19-20)

122. "God is our refuge and strength, a very present help in trouble. Therefore will not we fear, though the earth be removed, and though the mountains be carried into the midst of the sea." (Psalm 46:1-2)

123. "Be not afraid of their faces: for I am with thee to deliver thee, saith the Lord." (Jeremiah 1:8)

124. "And thou, son of man, be not afraid of them, neither be afraid of their words, though briers and thorns be with thee, and thou dost dwell among scorpions: be not afraid of their words, nor be dismayed at their looks, though they be a rebellious house." (Ezekiel 2:6)

125. "And now, Israel, what doth the Lord thy God require of thee, but to fear the Lord thy God, to walk in all his ways, and to love him, and to serve the Lord thy God with all thy heart and with all thy soul." (Deuteronomy 10:12)

126. "But when Jesus heard it, he answered him, saying, Fear not: believe only, and she shall be made whole." (Luke 8:50)

127. "Moreover thou shalt provide out of all the people able men, such as fear God, men of truth, hating covetousness; and place such over them, to be rulers of thousands, and rulers of hundreds, rulers of fifties, and rulers of tens." (Exodus 18:21)

128. "Fear not, daughter of Sion: behold, thy King cometh, sitting on an ass's colt." (John 12:15)

129. "Wherefore I put thee in remembrance that thou stir up the gift of God, which is in thee by the putting on of my hands. For God hath not given us the spirit of fear; but of power, and of love, and of a sound mind." (2 Timothy 1:6-7)

130. "Moreover he said, I am the God of thy father, the God of Abraham, the God of Isaac, and the God of Jacob.
And Moses hid his face; for he was afraid to look upon God." (Exodus 3:6)

131. "Thou drewest near in the day that I called upon thee: thou saidst, Fear not." (Lamentations 3:57)

132. "By faith he forsook Egypt, not fearing the wrath of the king: for he endured, as seeing him who is invisible." (Hebrews 11:27)

133. "Let us therefore fear, lest, a promise being left us of entering into his rest, any of you should seem to come short of it." (Hebrews 4:1)

134. "The fear of the Lord is the beginning of wisdom: and the knowledge of the holy is understanding." (Proverbs 9:10)

135. "And Jesus came and touched them, and said, Arise, and be not afraid." (Matthew 17:7)

136. "And the angel answered and said unto the women, Fear not ye: for I know that ye seek Jesus, which was crucified." (Matthew 28:5)

137. "Fear them not therefore: for there is nothing covered, that shall not be revealed; and hid, that shall not be known." (Matthew 10:26)

138. "Then said Jesus unto them, Be not afraid: go tell my brethren that they go into Galilee, and there shall they see me." (Matthew 28:10)

139. "I, even I, am he that comforteth you: who art thou, that thou shouldest be afraid of a man that shall die, and of the son of man which shall be made as grass." (Isaiah 51:12)

140. "And many of the brethren in the Lord, waxing confident by my bonds, are much more bold to speak the word without fear." (Philippians 1:14)

141. "And when Saul saw the host of the Philistines, he was afraid, and his heart greatly trembled." (1 Samuel 28:5)

142. "And say unto him, Take heed, and be quiet; fear not, neither be fainthearted for the two tails of these smoking firebrands, for the fierce anger of Rezin with Syria, and of the son of Remaliah." (Isaiah 7:4)

143. "Be not afraid of the king of Babylon, of whom ye are afraid; be not afraid of him, saith the Lord: for I am with you to save you, and to deliver you from his hand." (Jeremiah 42:11)

144. "And the king said unto her, Be not afraid: for what sawest thou? And the woman said unto Saul, I saw gods ascending out of the earth." (1 Samuel 28:13)

145. "There was a certain man in Caesarea called Cornelius, a centurion of the band called the Italian band, A devout man, and one that feared God with all his house, which gave much alms to the people, and prayed to God always." (Acts 10:1-2)

146. "And when Pharaoh drew nigh, the children of Israel lifted up their eyes, and, behold, the Egyptians marched after them; and they were sore afraid: and the children of Israel cried out unto the Lord." (Exodus 14:10)

147. "Then went the captain with the officers, and brought them without violence: for they feared the people, lest they should have been stoned." (Acts 5:26)

148. "Then spake the Lord to Paul in the night by a vision, Be not afraid, but speak, and hold not thy peace: For I am with thee, and no man shall set on thee to hurt thee: for I have much people in this city." (Act 18:9-10)

149. "And he was afraid, and said, How dreadful is this place! this is none other but the house of God, and this is the gate of heaven." (Genesis 28:17)

150. "And it shall be to me a name of joy, a praise and an honour before all the nations of the earth, which shall hear all the good that I do unto them: and they shall fear and tremble for all the goodness and for all the prosperity that I procure unto it." (Jeremiah 33:9)

151. "But I will deliver thee in that day, saith the Lord: and thou shalt not be given into the hand of the men of whom thou art afraid." (Jeremiah 39:17)

152. "Are not five sparrows sold for two farthings, and not one of them is forgotten before God? But even the very hairs of your head are all numbered. Fear not therefore: ye are of more value than many sparrows." (Luke 12:6-7)

153. "Therefore shall the strong people glorify thee, the city of the terrible nations shall fear thee." (Isaiah 25:3)

154. "They that fear thee will be glad when they see me; because I have hoped in thy word." (Psalm 119:74)

155. "Also when they shall be afraid of that which is high, and fears shall be in the way, and the almond tree shall flourish, and the grasshopper shall be a burden, and desire shall fail: because man goeth to his long home, and the mourners go about the streets." (Ecclesiastes 12:5)

156. "And Isaiah said unto them, Thus shall ye say to your master, Thus saith the Lord, Be not afraid of the words which thou hast heard, with which the servants of the king of Assyria have blasphemed me." (2 Kings 19:6)

157. "Dominion and fear are with him, he maketh peace in his high places." (Job 25:2)

158. "Then hear thou from the heavens, even from thy dwelling place, and do according to all that the stranger calleth to thee for; that all people of the earth may know thy name, and fear thee, as doth thy people Israel, and may know that this house which I have built is called by thy name." (2 Chronicles 6:33)

159. "He will bless them that fear the Lord, both small and great." (Psalm 115:13)

160. "Ye that fear the Lord, praise him; all ye the seed of Jacob, glorify him; and fear him, all ye the seed of Israel." (Psalm 22:23)

161. "My praise shall be of thee in the great congregation: I will pay my vows before them that fear him." (Psalm 22:25)

162. "Only fear the Lord, and serve him in truth with all your heart: for consider how great things he hath done for you." (1 Samuel 12:24)

163. "Men's hearts failing them for fear, and for looking after those things which are coming on the earth: for the powers of heaven shall be shaken."
(Luke 21:26)

164. "He shall not be afraid of evil tidings: his heart is fixed, trusting in the Lord. His heart is established, he shall not be afraid, until he see his desire upon his enemies." (Psalm 112:7-8)

165. "Deliver me, I pray thee, from the hand of my brother, from the hand of Esau: for I fear him, lest he will come and smite me, and the mother with the children." (Genesis 32:11)

166. "O Lord, I have heard thy speech, and was afraid:
O Lord, revive thy work in the midst of the years,
in the midst of the years make known; in wrath
remember mercy." (Habakkuk 3:2)

167. "When a prophet speaketh in the name of the Lord,
if the thing follow not, nor come to pass, that is
the thing which the Lord hath not spoken, but the
prophet hath spoken it presumptuously: thou shalt
not be afraid of him." (Deuteronomy 18:22)

168. "I will send my fear before thee, and will destroy all
the people to whom thou shalt come, and I will make
all thine enemies turn their backs unto thee."
(Exodus 23:27)

169. "But fear not thou, O my servant Jacob, and be not dismayed, O Israel: for, behold, I will save thee from afar off, and thy seed from the land of their captivity; and Jacob shall return, and be in rest and at ease, and none shall make him afraid." (Jeremiah 46:27)

170. "Thou shalt not curse the deaf, nor put a stumbling block before the blind, but shalt fear thy God: I am the Lord." (Leviticus 19:14)

171. "Thou shalt rise up before the hoary head, and honour the face of the old man, and fear thy God: I am the Lord." (Leviticus 19:32)

172. "And that their children, which have not known any thing, may hear, and learn to fear the Lord your God, as long as ye live in the land whither ye go over Jordan to possess it." (Deuteronomy 31:13)

173. "He saw in a vision evidently about the ninth hour of the day an angel of God coming into him, and saying unto him, Cornelius. And when he looked on him, he was afraid, and said, What is it, Lord? And he said unto him, Thy prayers and thine alms are come up for a memorial before God." (Acts 10:3-4)

174. "By faith Moses, when he was born, was hid three months of his parents, because they saw he was a proper child; and they were not afraid of the king's commandment." (Hebrews 11:23)

175. "But the angel said unto him, Fear not, Zacharias: for thy prayer is heard; and thy wife Elisabeth shall bear thee a son, and thou shalt call his name John. And thou shalt have joy and gladness; and many shall rejoice at his birth." (Luke 1:13-14)

176. "Now if Timotheus come, see that he may be with you without fear: for he worketh the work of the Lord, as I also do." (1 Corinthians 16:10)

177. "I said, Surely thou wilt fear me, thou wilt receive instruction; so their dwelling should not be cut off, howsoever I punished them: but they rose early, and corrupted all their doings." (Zephaniah 3:7)

178. "Thou shalt not be afraid for the terror by night; nor for the arrow that flieth by day; Nor for the pestilence that walketh in darkness; nor for the destruction that wasteth at noonday." (Psalm 91:5-6)

179. "And Elihu the son of Barachel the Buzite answered and said, I am young, and ye are very old; wherefore I was afraid, and durst not shew you mine opinion." (Job 32:6)

180. "God shall hear, and afflict them, even he that abideth of old. Selah. Because they have no changes, therefore they fear not God." (Psalm 55:19)

181. "Also I said, It is not good that ye do: ought ye not to walk in the fear of our God because of the reproach of the heathen our enemies?" (Nehemiah 5:9)

182. "How he met thee by the way, and smote the hindmost of thee, even all that were feeble behind thee, when thou wast faint and weary; and he feared not God." (Deuteronomy 25:18)

183. "But the former governors that had been before me were chargeable unto the people, and had taken of them bread and wine, beside forty shekels of silver; yea, even their servants bare rule over the people: but so did not I, because of the fear of God." (Nehemiah 5:15)

184. "And if we have not rather done it for fear of this thing, saying, In time to come your children might speak unto our children, saying, What have ye to do with the Lord God of Israel? For the Lord hath made Jordan a border between us and you, ye children of Reuben and children of Gad; ye have no part in the Lord: so shall your children make our children cease from fearing the Lord." (Joshua 22:24-25)

185. "Unto this day they do after the former manners: they fear not the Lord, neither do they after their statutes, or after their ordinances, or after the law and commandment which the Lord commanded the children of Jacob, whom he named Israel." (2 Kings 17:34)

186. "Behold, the eye of the Lord is upon them that fear him, upon them that hope in his mercy." (Psalm 33:18)

187. "But it shall not be well with the wicked, neither shall he prolong his days, which are as a shadow; because he feareth not before God." (Ecclesiastes 8:13)

188. "For now they shall say, We have no king, because we feared not the Lord; what then should a king do to us?" (Hosea 10:3)

189. "Saying, There was in a city a judge, which feared not God, neither regarded man." (Luke 18:2)

190. "And he would not for a while: but afterward he said within himself, Though I fear not God, nor regard man." (Luke 18:4)

191. "Servants, be subject to your masters with all fear; not only to the good and gentle, but also to the froward." (1 Peter 2:18)

192. "And the fame of David went out into all lands; and the Lord brought the fear of him upon all nations." (1 Chronicles 14:17)

193. "But as for thee and thy servants, I know that ye will not yet fear the Lord God." (Exodus 9:30)

194. "Thine own wickedness shall correct thee, and thy backslidings shall reprove thee: know therefore and see that it is an evil thing and bitter, that thou hast forsaken the Lord thy God, and that my fear is not in thee, saith the Lord God of hosts." (Jeremiah 2:19)

195. "They are not humbled even unto this day, neither have they feared, nor walked in my law, nor in my statutes, that I set before you and before your fathers." (Jeremiah 44:10)

196. "And Ananias hearing these words fell down, and gave up the ghost: and great fear came on all them that heard these things." (Acts 5:5)

197. "But the other answering rebuked him, saying, Dost not thou fear God, seeing thou art in the same condemnation?" (Luke 23:40)

198. "And Abraham said, Because I thought, Surely the fear of God is not in this place; and they will slay me for my wife's sake." (Genesis 20:11)

199. "And unto man he said, Behold, the fear of the Lord, that is wisdom; and to depart from evil is understanding." (Job 28:28)

200. "In whose eyes a vile person is contemned; but he honoureth them that fear the Lord. He that sweareth to his own hurt, and changeth not." (Psalm 15:4)

201. "Ye that fear the Lord, trust in the Lord: he is their help and their shield." (Psalm 115:11)

202. "And the Lord said unto Satan, Hast thou considered my servant Job, that there is none like him in the earth, a perfect and an upright man, one that feareth God, and escheweth evil? Then Satan answered the Lord, and said, Doth Job fear God for nought?" (Job 1:8-9)

203. "The fear of the Lord is the beginning of wisdom: a good understanding have all they that do his commandments: his praise endureth for ever." (Psalm 111:10)

204. "Men do therefore fear him: he respecteth not any that are wise of heart." (Job 37:24)

205. "But the mercy of the Lord is from everlasting to everlasting upon them that fear him, and his righteousness unto children's children." (Psalm 103:17)

206. "Serve the Lord with fear, and rejoice with trembling." (Psalm 2:11)

207. "God shall bless us; and all the ends of the earth shall fear him." (Psalm 67:7)

208. "Better is little with the fear of the Lord than great treasure and trouble therewith." (Proverbs 15:16)

209. "But as for me, I will come into thy house in the multitude of thy mercy: and in thy fear will I worship toward thy holy temple." (Psalm 5:7)

210. "And he said, Lay not thine hand upon the lad, neither do thou any thing unto him: for now I know that thou fearest God, seeing thou hast not withheld thy son, thine only son from me." (Genesis 22:12)

211. "And the fear of the Lord fell upon all the kingdoms of the lands that were round about Judah, so that they made no war against Jehoshaphat."
(2 Chronicles 17:10)

212. "If ye will fear the Lord, and serve him, and obey his voice, and not rebel against the commandment of the Lord, then shall both ye and also the king that reigneth over you continue following the Lord your God." (1 Samuel 12:14)

213. "Praise ye the Lord. Blessed is the man that feareth the Lord, that delighteth greatly in his commandments."
(Psalm 112:1)

214. "And he said unto his brethren, My money is restored; and, lo, it is even in my sack: and their heart failed them, and they were afraid, saying one to another, What is this that God hath done unto us?" (Genesis 42:28)

215. "And the serjeants told these words unto the magistrates: and they feared, when they heard that they were Romans." (Acts 16:38)

216. "Now therefore fear the Lord, and serve him in sincerity and in truth: and put away the gods which your fathers served on the other side of the flood, and in Egypt; and serve ye the Lord." (Joshua 24:14)

217. The fear of the Lord is to hate evil: pride, and arrogancy, and the evil way, and the froward mouth, do I hate." (Proverbs 8:13)

218. "Then had the churches rest throughout all Judaea and Galilee and Samaria, and were edified; and walking in the fear of the Lord, and in the comfort of the Holy Ghost, were multiplied." (Acts 9:31)

219. "The fear of the Lord is clean, enduring for ever: the judgments of the Lord are true and righteous altogether." (Psalm 19:9)

220. "Then Paul stood up, and beckoning with his hand said, Men of Israel, and ye that fear God, give audience." (Acts 13:16)

221. "And there came a fear on all: and they glorified God, saying, That a great prophet is risen up among us; and, That God hath visited his people." (Luke 7:16)

222. "Wherefore we receiving a kingdom which cannot be moved, let us have grace, whereby we may serve God acceptably with reverence and godly fear: For our God is a consuming fire." (Hebrews 12:28-29)

223. "When the waves of death compassed me, the floods of ungodly men made me afraid." (2 Samuel 22:5)

224. "My son, fear thou the Lord and the king: and meddle not with them that are given to change."
(Proverbs 24:21)

225. "The fear of the Lord is the beginning of knowledge: but fools despise wisdom and instruction."
(Proverbs 1:7)

226. "The fear of the Lord is the instruction of wisdom; and before honour is humility." (Proverbs 15:33)

227. "The fear of the Lord prolongeth days: but the years of the wicked shall be shortened." (Proverbs 10:27)

228. "The fear of the Lord is a fountain of life, to depart from the snares of death." (Proverbs 14:27)

229. "And wisdom and knowledge shall be the stability of thy times, and strength of salvation: the fear of the Lord is his treasure." (Isaiah 33:6)

230. "In the fear of the Lord is strong confidence: and his children shall have a place of refuge." (Proverbs 14:26)

231. "Is not this thy fear, thy confidence, thy hope, and the uprightness of thy ways?" (Job 4:6)

232. "He that walketh in his uprightness feareth the Lord: but he that is perverse in his ways despiseth him." (Proverbs 14:2)

233. "Let not thine heart envy sinners: but be thou in the fear of the Lord all the day long." (Proverbs 23:17)

234. "Let all the earth fear the Lord: let all the inhabitants of the world stand in awe of him." (Psalm 33:8)

235. "And thou shalt eat before the Lord thy God, in the place which he shall choose to place his name there, the tithe of thy corn, of thy wine, and of thine oil, and the firstlings of thy herds and of thy flocks; that thou mayest learn to fear the Lord thy God always." (Deuteronomy 14:23)

236. "Servants, obey in all things your masters according to the flesh; not with eyeservice, as menpleasers; but in singleness of heart, fearing God." (Colossians 3:22)

237. "Come, ye children, hearken unto me: I will teach you the fear of the Lord." (Psalm 34:11)

238. "The angel of the Lord encampeth round about them that fear him, and delivereth them." (Psalm 34:7)

239. "And David was afraid of the Lord that day, and said, How shall the ark of the Lord come to me?" (2 Samuel 6:9)

240. "And when I saw him, I fell at his feet as dead. And he laid his right hand upon me, saying unto me, Fear not; I am the first and the last." (Revelation 1:17)

241. "Oh how great is thy goodness, which thou hast laid up for them that fear thee; which thou hast wrought for them that trust in thee before the sons of men!" (Psalm 31:19)

242. "And David said unto him, How wast thou not afraid to stretch forth thine hand to destroy the Lord's anointed?" (2 Samuel 1:14)

243. "By mercy and truth iniquity is purged: and by the fear of the Lord men depart from evil." (Proverbs 16:6)

244. "And he said, I heard thy voice in the garden, and I was afraid, because I was naked; and I hid myself." (Genesis 3:10)

245. "And when the Philistines heard that the children of Israel were gathered together to Mizpeh, the lords of the Philistines went up against Israel. And when the children of Israel heard it, they were afraid of the Philistines." (1 Samuel 7:7)

246. "Whither shall we go up? our brethren have discouraged our heart, saying, The people is greater and taller than we; the cities are great and walled up to heaven; and moreover we have seen the sons of the Anakims there. Then I said unto you, Dread not, neither be afraid of them." (Deuteronomy 1:28-29)

247. "Now therefore go to, proclaim in the ears of the people, saying, Whosoever is fearful and afraid, let him return and depart early from mount Gilead. And there returned of the people twenty and two thousand; and there remained ten thousand." (Judges 7:3)

248. "And the Philistines were afraid, for they said, God is come into the camp. And they said, Woe unto us! for there hath not been such a thing heretofore." (1 Samuel 4:7)

249. "And Elijah said unto her, Fear not; go and do as thou hast said: but make me thereof a little cake first, and bring it unto me, and after make for thee and for thy son." (1 Kings 17:13)

250. "O Lord, why hast thou made us to err from thy ways, and hardened our heart from thy fear? Return for thy servants' sake, the tribes of thine inheritance." (Isaiah 63:17)

251. "So shall they fear the name of the Lord from the west, and his glory from the rising of the sun. When the enemy shall come in like a flood, the Spirit of the Lord shall lift up a standard against him." (Isaiah 59:19)

252. "And all the people, both small and great, and the captains of the armies, arose, and came to Egypt: for they were afraid of the Chaldees." (2 Kings 25:26)

253. "And David was afraid of God that day, saying, How shall I bring the ark of God home to me?" (1 Chronicles 13:12)

254. "And they set the altar upon his bases; for fear was upon them because of the people of those countries: and they offered burnt offerings thereon unto the Lord, even burnt offerings morning and evening." (Ezra 3:3)

255. "The Jews gathered themselves together in their cities throughout all the provinces of the king Ahasuerus, to lay hand on such as sought their hurt: and no man could withstand them; for the fear of them fell upon all people." (Esther 9:2)

256. "And all the rulers of the provinces, and the lieutenants, and the deputies, and officers of the king, helped the Jews; because the fear of Mordecai fell upon them." (Esther 9:3)

257. "Behold, happy is the man whom God correcteth: therefore despise not thou the chastening of the Almighty: For he maketh sore, and bindeth up: he woundeth, and his hands make whole. He shall deliver thee in six troubles: yea, in seven there shall no evil touch thee. In famine he shall redeem thee from death: and in war from the power of the sword. Thou shalt be hid from the scourge of the tongue: neither shalt thou be afraid of destruction when it cometh. At destruction and famine thou shalt laugh: neither shalt thou be afraid of the beasts of the earth." (Job 5:17-22)

258. "Thou, even thou, art to be feared: and who may stand in thy sight when once thou art angry? Thou didst cause judgment to be heard from heaven; the earth feared, and was still." (Psalm 76:7-8)

259. "The days of our years are threescore years and ten; and if by reason of strength they be fourscore years, yet is their strength labour and sorrow; for it is soon cut off, and we fly away. Who knoweth the power of thine anger? even according to thy fear, so is thy wrath. So teach us to number our days, that we may apply our hearts unto wisdom." (Psalm 90:10-12)

260. "My flesh trembleth for fear of thee; and I am afraid of thy judgments." (Psalm 119:120)

261. "For the turning away of the simple shall slay them, and the prosperity of fools shall destroy them. But whoso hearkeneth unto me shall dwell safely, and shall be quiet from fear of evil." (Proverbs 1:32-33)

262. "Say ye not, A confederacy, to all them to whom this people shall say, A confederacy; neither fear ye their fear, nor be afraid. Sanctify the Lord of hosts himself; and let him be your fear, and let him be your dread." (Isaiah 8:12-13)

263. "God is greatly to be feared in the assembly of the saints, and to be had in reverence of all them that are about him." (Psalm 89:7)

264. "Behold, God is my salvation; I will trust, and not be afraid: for the Lord Jehovah is my strength and my song; he also is become my salvation. Therefore with joy shall ye draw water out of the wells of salvation." (Isaiah 12:2-3)

265. "Fear not; for thou shalt not be ashamed: neither be thou confounded; for thou shalt not be put to shame: for thou shalt forget the shame of thy youth, and shalt not remember the reproach of thy widowhood any more.
For thy Maker is thine husband; the Lord of hosts is his name; and thy Redeemer the Holy One of Israel; The God of the whole earth shall he be called." (Isaiah 54:4-5)

266. "And of whom hast thou been afraid or feared, that thou hast lied, and hast not remembered me, nor laid it to thy heart? have not I held my peace even of old, and thou fearest me not?" (Isaiah 57:11)

267. "I also will choose their delusions, and will bring their fears upon them; because when I called, none did answer; when I spake, they did not hear: but they did evil before mine eyes, and chose that in which I delighted not." (Isaiah 66:4)

268. "Go not forth into the field, nor walk by the way; for the sword of the enemy and fear is on every side." (Jeremiah 6:25)

269. "For I heard the defaming of many, fear on every side. Report, say they, and we will report it. All my familiars watched for my halting, saying, Peradventure he will be enticed, and we shall prevail against him, and we shall take our revenge on him." (Jeremiah 20:10)

270. "Then it shall come to pass, that the sword, which ye feared, shall overtake you there in the land of Egypt, and the famine, whereof ye were afraid, shall follow close after you there in Egypt; and there ye shall die." (Jeremiah 42:16)

271. "Wherefore have I seen them dismayed and turned away back? and their mighty ones are beaten down, and are fled apace, and look not back: for fear was round about, saith the Lord." (Jeremiah 46:5)

272. "Stablish thy word unto thy servant, who is devoted to thy fear." (Psalm 119:38)

273. "And he said, Come. And when Peter was come down out of the ship, he walked on the water, to go to Jesus. But when he saw the wind boisterous, he was afraid; and beginning to sink, he cried, saying, Lord, save me. And immediately Jesus stretched forth his hand, and caught him, and said unto him, O thou of little faith, wherefore didst thou doubt?" (Matthew 14:29-31)

274. "God is greatly to be feared in the assembly of the saints, and to be had in reverence of all them that are about him." (Psalm 36:1)

275. "And the land of Judah shall be a terror unto Egypt, every one that maketh mention thereof shall be afraid in himself, because of the counsel of the Lord of hosts, which he hath determined against it."
(Isaiah 19:17)

276. "And he arose, and rebuked the wind, and said unto the sea, Peace, be still. And the wind ceased, and there was a great calm. And he said unto them, Why are ye so fearful? how is it that ye have no faith? And they feared exceedingly, and said one to another, What manner of man is this, that even the wind and the sea obey him?" (Mark 4:39-41)

277. "There were they in great fear: for God is in the generation of the righteous." (Psalm 14:5)

278. "When Simon Peter saw it, he fell down at Jesus' knees, saying, Depart from me; for I am a sinful man, O Lord. For he was astonished, and all that were with him, at the draught of the fishes which they had taken: And so was also James, and John, the sons of Zebedee, which were partners with Simon. And Jesus said unto Simon, Fear not; from henceforth thou shalt catch men."
(Luke 5:8-10)

279. "Put them in fear, O Lord: that the nations may know themselves to be but men. Selah." (Psalm 9:20)

280. "The Lord knoweth how to deliver the godly out of temptations, and to reserve the unjust unto the day of judgment to be punished: But chiefly them that walk after the flesh in the lust of uncleanness, and despise government. Presumptuous are they, selfwilled, they are not afraid to speak evil of dignities. Whereas angels, which are greater in power and might, bring not railing accusation against them before the Lord." (2 Peter 2:9-11)

281. "And after three days and an half the spirit of life from God entered into them, and they stood upon their feet; and great fear fell upon them which saw them." (Revelation 11:11)

282. "The fear of the wicked, it shall come upon him: but the desire of the righteous shall be granted." (Proverbs 10:24)

283. "And I was with you in weakness, and in fear, and in much trembling." (1 Corinthians 2:3)

284. "That he would grant unto us, that we being delivered out of the hand of our enemies might serve him without fear." (Luke 1:74)

285. "With whom the Lord had made a covenant, and charged them, saying, Ye shall not fear other gods, nor bow yourselves to them, nor serve them, nor sacrifice to them: But the Lord, who brought you up out of the land of Egypt with great power and a stretched out arm, him shall ye fear, and him shall ye worship, and to him shall ye do sacrifice. And the statutes, and the ordinances, and the law, and the commandment, which he wrote for you, ye shall observe to do for evermore; and ye shall not fear other gods. And the covenant that I have made with you ye shall not forget; neither shall ye fear other gods." (2 Kings 17:35-38)

286. "But the woman fearing and trembling, knowing what was done in her, came and fell down before him, and told him all the truth." (Mark 5:33)

287. "And all men shall fear, and shall declare the work of God; for they shall wisely consider of his doing." (Psalm 64:9)

288. "Behold, I will bring a fear upon thee, saith the Lord God of hosts, from all those that be about thee; and ye shall be driven out every man right forth; and none shall gather up him that wandereth." (Jeremiah 49:5)

289. "And they shall no more be a prey to the heathen, neither shall the beast of the land devour them; but they shall dwell safely, and none shall make them afraid." (Ezekiel 34:28)

290. "And he shall judge among many people, and rebuke strong nations afar off; and they shall beat their swords into plowshares, and their spears into pruninghooks: nation shall not lift up a sword against nation, neither shall they learn war anymore. But they shall sit every man under his vine and under his fig tree; and none shall make them afraid: for the mouth of the Lord of hosts hath spoken it." (Micah 4:3-4)

291. "For thus saith the Lord of hosts; As I thought to punish you, when your fathers provoked me to wrath, saith the Lord of hosts, and I repented not: So again have I thought in these days to do well unto Jerusalem and to the house of Judah: fear ye not." (Zechariah 8:14-15)

292. "And he saith unto them, Why are ye fearful, O ye of little faith? Then he arose, and rebuked the winds and the sea; and there was a great calm." (Matthew 8:26)

293. "I know that, whatsoever God doeth, it shall be for ever: nothing can be put to it, nor any thing taken from it: and God doeth it, that men should fear before him." (Ecclesiastes 3:14)

294. "By humility and the fear of the Lord are riches, and honour, and life." (Proverbs 22:4)

295. "Let us hear the conclusion of the whole matter: Fear God, and keep his commandments: for this is the whole duty of man." (Ecclesiastes 12:13)

296. "Behold, all his fellows shall be ashamed: and the workmen, they are of men: let them all be gathered together, let them stand up; yet they shall fear, and they shall be ashamed together." (Isaiah 44:11)

297. "That they feared greatly, because Gibeon was a great city, as one of the royal cities, and because it was greater than Ai, and all the men thereof were mighty." (Joshua 10:2)

298. "And lest your heart faint, and ye fear for the rumour that shall be heard in the land; a rumour shall both come one year, and after that in another year shall come a rumour, and violence in the land, ruler against ruler.
Therefore, behold, the days come, that I will do judgment upon the graven images of Babylon: and her whole land shall be confounded, and all her slain shall fall in the midst of her." (Jeremiah 51:46-47)

299. "And, behold, there was a great earthquake: for the angel of the Lord descended from heaven, and came and rolled back the stone from the door, and sat upon it. His countenance was like lightning, and his raiment white as snow: And for fear of him the keepers did shake, and became as dead men." (Matthew 28:2-4)

300. "For Herod feared John, knowing that he was a just man and an holy, and observed him; and when he heard him, he did many things, and heard him gladly." (Mark 6:20)

301. "And they were in the way going up to Jerusalem; and Jesus went before them: and they were amazed; and as they followed, they were afraid. And he took again the twelve, and began to tell them what things should happen unto him." (Mark 10:32)

302. "Shall not his excellency make you afraid? and his dread fall upon you?" (Job 13:11)

303. "Then they went out to see what was done; and came to Jesus, and found the man, out of whom the devils were departed, sitting at the feet of Jesus, clothed, and in his right mind: and they were afraid. They also which saw it told them by what means he that was possessed of the devils was healed. Then the whole multitude of the country of the Gadarenes round about besought him to depart from them; for they were taken with great fear: and he went up into the ship, and returned back again." (Luke 8:35-37)

304. "And it came to pass, as they were much perplexed thereabout, behold, two men stood by them in shining garments: And as they were afraid, and bowed down their faces to the earth, they said unto them, Why seek ye the living among the dead?" (Luke 24:4-5)

305. "Therefore thou shalt keep the commandments of the Lord thy God, to walk in his ways, and to fear him." (Deuteronomy 8:6)

306. "And the Lord commanded us to do all these statutes, to fear the Lord our God, for our good always, that he might preserve us alive, as it is at this day." (Deuteronomy 6:24)

307. "Thou shalt fear the Lord thy God, and serve him, and shalt swear by his name. Ye shall not go after other gods, of the gods of the people which are round about you." (Deuteronomy 6:13-14)

308. "And the Lord heard the voice of your words, when ye spake unto me; and the Lord said unto me, I have heard the voice of the words of this people, which they have spoken unto thee: they have well said all that they have spoken. O that there were such an heart in them, that they would fear me, and keep all my commandments always, that it might be well with them, and with their children for ever!" (Deuteronomy 5:28-29)

309. "And I saw another angel fly in the midst of heaven, having the everlasting gospel to preach unto them that dwell on the earth, and to every nation, and kindred, and tongue, and people, Saying with a loud voice, Fear God, and give glory to him; for the hour of his judgment is come: and worship him that made

heaven, and earth, and the sea, and the fountains of waters." (Revelation 14:6-7)

310. "And they sing the song of Moses the servant of God, and the song of the Lamb, saying, Great and marvellous are thy works, Lord God Almighty; just and true are thy ways, thou King of saints. Who shall not fear thee, O Lord, and glorify thy name? for thou only art holy: for all nations shall come and worship before thee; for thy judgments are made manifest." (Revelation 15:3-4)

311. "And I will set up shepherds over them which shall feed them: and they shall fear no more, nor be dismayed, neither shall they be lacking, saith the Lord." (Jeremiah 23:4)

312. "Who would not fear thee, O King of nations? for to thee doth it appertain: forasmuch as among all the wise men of the nations, and in all their kingdoms, there is none like unto thee. But they are altogether brutish and foolish: the stock is a doctrine of vanities." (Jeremiah 10:7-8)

313. "The Lord taketh pleasure in them that fear him, in those that hope in his mercy." (Psalm 147:11)

314. "He will fulfil the desire of them that fear him: he also will hear their cry, and will save them." (Psalm 145:19)

315. "Bless the Lord, O house of Levi: ye that fear the Lord, bless the Lord. Blessed be the Lord out of Zion, which dwelleth at Jerusalem. Praise ye the Lord." (Psalm 135:20-21)

316. "Blessed is every one that feareth the Lord; that walketh in his ways. For thou shalt eat the labour of thine hands: happy shalt thou be, and it shall be well with thee. Thy wife shall be as a fruitful vine by the sides of thine house: thy children like olive plants round about thy table. Behold, that thus shall the man be blessed that feareth the Lord." (Psalm 128:1-4)

317. "And he charged them, saying, Thus shall ye do in the fear of the Lord, faithfully, and with a perfect heart." (2 Chronicles 19:9)

318. "And his inward affection is more abundant toward you, whilst he remembereth the obedience of you all, how with fear and trembling ye received him." (2 Corinthians 7:15)

319. "But the Lord, who brought you up out of the land of Egypt with great power and a stretched out arm, him shall ye fear, and him shall ye worship, and to him shall ye do sacrifice." (2 Chronicles 19:7)

320. "And Joseph said unto them the third day, This do, and live; for I fear God." (Genesis 42:18)

321. "For as the heaven is high above the earth, so great is his mercy toward them that fear him." (Psalm 103:11)

322. "And the prince of the eunuchs said unto Daniel, I fear my lord the king, who hath appointed your meat and your drink: for why should he see your faces worse liking than the children which are of your sort? then shall ye make me endanger my head to the king." (Daniel 1:10)

323. "I make a decree, That in every dominion of my kingdom men tremble and fear before the God of Daniel: for he is the living God, and stedfast for ever, and his kingdom that which shall not be destroyed, and his dominion shall be even unto the end." (Daniel 6:26)

324. "Shall a trumpet be blown in the city, and the people not be afraid? shall there be evil in a city, and the Lord hath not done it? Surely the Lord God will do nothing, but he revealeth his secret unto his servants the prophets. The lion hath roared, who will not fear? the Lord God hath spoken, who can but prophesy?" (Amos 3:6-8)

325. "Then the mariners were afraid, and cried every man unto his god, and cast forth the wares that were in the ship into the sea, to lighten it of them. But Jonah was gone down into the sides of the ship; and he lay, and was fast asleep." (Jonah 1:5)

326. "And he said unto them, I am an Hebrew; and I fear the Lord, the God of heaven, which hath made the sea and the dry land." (Jonah 1:9)

327. "And this was known to all the Jews and Greeks also dwelling at Ephesus; and fear fell on them all, and the name of the Lord Jesus was magnified." (Acts 19:17)

328. "The nations shall see and be confounded at all their might: they shall lay their hand upon their mouth, their ears shall be deaf. They shall lick the dust like a serpent, they shall move out of their holes like worms of the earth: they shall be afraid of the Lord our God, and shall fear because of thee." (Micah 7:16-17)

329. "Then Zerubbabel the son of Shealtiel, and Joshua the son of Josedech, the high priest, with all the remnant of the people, obeyed the voice of the Lord their God, and the words of Haggai the prophet, as the Lord their God had sent him, and the people did fear before the Lord." (Haggai 1:12)

330. "And ye shall know that I have sent this commandment unto you, that my covenant might be with Levi, saith the Lord of hosts. My covenant was with him of life and peace; and I gave them to him for the fear wherewith he feared me, and was afraid before my name." (Malachi 2:4-5)

331. "Then they that feared the Lord spake often one to another: and the Lord hearkened, and heard it, and a book of remembrance was written before him for them that feared the Lord, and that thought upon his name. And they shall be mine, saith the Lord of hosts, in that day when I make up my jewels; and I will spare them, as a man spareth his own son that serveth him. Then shall ye return, and discern between the righteous and the wicked, between him that serveth God and him that serveth him not." (Malachi 3:16-18)

332. "But unto you that fear my name shall the Sun of righteousness arise with healing in his wings; and ye shall go forth, and grow up as calves of the stall." (Malachi 4:2)

333. "For rulers are not a terror to good works, but to the evil. Wilt thou then not be afraid of the power? do that which is good, and thou shalt have praise of the same: For he is the minister of God to thee for good. But if thou do that which is evil, be afraid; for he beareth not the sword in vain: for he is the minister of God, a revenger to execute wrath upon him that doeth evil." (Romans 13:3-4)

334. "And I said, Should such a man as I flee? and who is
there, that, being as I am, would go into the temple
to save his life? I will not go in. And, lo, I perceived
that God had not sent him; but that he pronounced
this prophecy against me: for Tobiah and Sanballat
had hired him. Therefore was he hired, that I should
be afraid, and do so, and sin, and that they might have
matter for an evil report, that they might reproach
me." (Nehemiah 6:11-13)

335. "But unto you that fear my name shall the Sun
of righteousness arise with healing in his wings;
and ye shall go forth, and grow up as calves of the
stall." (Nehemiah 6:9)

336. "And when Saul was come to Jerusalem, he assayed to
join himself to the disciples: but they were all afraid
of him, and believed not that he was a disciple."
(Acts 9:26)

337. "And it came to pass the same night, that the Lord said unto him, Arise, get thee down unto the host; for I have delivered it into thine hand. But if thou fear to go down, go thou with Phurah thy servant down to the host: And thou shalt hear what they say; and afterward shall thine hands be strengthened to go down unto the host. Then went he down with Phurah his servant unto the outside of the armed men that were in the host." (Judges 7:9-11)

338. "And the officers shall speak further unto the people, and they shall say, What man is there that is fearful and fainthearted? let him go and return unto his house, lest his brethren's heart faint as well as his heart." (Deuteronomy 20:8)

339. "Withdraw thine hand far from me: and let not thy dread make me afraid." (Job 13:21)

340. "And they sought to lay hold on him, but feared the people: for they knew that he had spoken the parable against them: and they left him, and went their way."   (Mark 12:12)

341. "And the scribes and chief priests heard it, and sought how they might destroy him: for they feared him, because all the people was astonished at his doctrine." (Mark 11:18)

342. "But if we shall say, Of men; they feared the people: for all men counted John, that he was a prophet indeed. And they answered and said unto Jesus, We cannot tell. And Jesus answering saith unto them, Neither do I tell you by what authority I do these things."
(Mark 11:32-33)

343. "For he taught his disciples, and said unto them, The Son of man is delivered into the hands of men, and they shall kill him; and after that he is killed, he shall rise the third day. But they understood not that saying, and were afraid to ask him." (Mark 9:31-32)

344. "There is no fear of God before their eyes." (Romans 3:18)

345. "That they may fear thee, to walk in thy ways, so long as they live in the land which thou gavest unto our fathers." (2 Chronicles 6:31)

346. "But the Lord your God ye shall fear; and he shall deliver you out of the hand of all your enemies."

(2 Kings 17:39)

347. "And it shall come to pass, as soon as I am gone from thee, that the Spirit of the Lord shall carry thee whither I know not; and so when I come and tell Ahab, and he cannot find thee, he shall slay me: but I thy servant fear the Lord from my youth." (1 Kings 18:12)

348. "And Saul was afraid of David, because the Lord was with him, and was departed from Saul."
(1 Samuel 18:12)

349. "And all the men of Israel, when they saw the man, fled from him, and were sore afraid." (1 Samuel 17:24)

350. "And they answered Joshua, and said, Because it was certainly told thy servants, how that the Lord thy God commanded his servant Moses to give you all the land, and to destroy all the inhabitants of the land from before you, therefore we were sore afraid of our lives because of you, and have done this thing." (Joshua 9:24)

351. "That all the people of the earth might know the hand of the Lord, that it is mighty: that ye might fear the Lord your God for ever." (Joshua 4:24)

352. "Gather the people together, men and women, and children, and thy stranger that is within thy gates, that they may hear, and that they may learn, and fear the Lord your God, and observe to do all the words of this law." (Deuteronomy 31:12)

353. "If thou wilt not observe to do all the words of this law that are written in this book, that thou mayest fear this glorious and fearful name, The Lord Thy God." (Deuteronomy 28:58)

354. "And all people of the earth shall see that thou art called by the name of the Lord; and they shall be afraid of thee." (Deuteronomy 28:10)

355. "O taste and see that the Lord is good: blessed is the man that trusteth in him. O fear the Lord, ye his saints: for there is no want to them that fear him." (Psalm 34:8-9)

356. "And I will make an everlasting covenant with them, that I will not turn away from them, to do them good; but I will put my fear in their hearts, that they shall not depart from me. Yea, I will rejoice over them to do them good, and I will plant them in this land assuredly with my whole heart and with my whole soul." (Jeremiah 32:40-41)

357. "Now when the centurion, and they that were with him, watching Jesus, saw the earthquake, and those things that were done, they feared greatly, saying, Truly this was the Son of God." (Matthew 27:54)

358. "And they were all amazed, and they glorified God, and were filled with fear, saying, We have seen strange things today." (Luke 5:26)

359. "Having therefore these promises, dearly beloved, let us cleanse ourselves from all filthiness of the flesh and spirit, perfecting holiness in the fear of God." (2 Corinthians 7:1)

360. "In all thy ways acknowledge him, and he shall direct thy paths. Be not wise in thine own eyes: fear the Lord, and depart from evil." (Proverbs 3:6-7)

361. "So that thou incline thine ear unto wisdom, and apply thine heart to understanding; Yea, if thou criest after knowledge, and liftest up thy voice for understanding; If thou seekest her as silver, and searchest for her as for hid treasures; Then shalt thou understand the fear of the Lord, and find the knowledge of God." (Proverbs 2:2-5)

362. "Let them now that fear the Lord say, that his mercy endureth for ever." (Psalm 118:4)

363. "Honour all men. Love the brotherhood. Fear God. Honour the king." (1 Peter 2:17)

364. "They shall fear thee as long as the sun and moon endure, throughout all generations." (Psalm 72:5)

365. "Hear thou in heaven thy dwelling place, and do according to all that the stranger calleth to thee for: that all people of the earth may know thy name, to fear thee, as do thy people Israel; and that they may know that this house, which I have builded, is called by thy name." (1 Kings 8:43)

Made in United States
Troutdale, OR
02/06/2024

17508319R00075